TEKLA

An Urban Winter's Tale

THOM HUERTH

 page vision

228 Hamilton Ave.,
Palo Alto, CA 94301

RECIPE FOR MANHATTAN

INGREDIENTS:

2 ounces bourbon or *rye* whisky
1 ounce sweet vermouth
2 or 3 dashes aromatic bitters
Preserved cherry, for garnish

INSTRUCTIONS:

Chill a cocktail glass. Half fill a cocktail shaker with ice. Add whisky, vermouth, and bitters. Stir well. Strain into glass. Add cherry before serving.

PROLOGUE

Dear Reader,

I hope you enjoy this story and that you may be able to capture for yourself something of the essence of the character I have tried to put down in this endeavor.

Have you ever met a person in your life that you could never quite forget? Someone so singular that even after they are gone from this life, they seem to infiltrate your awareness in little ways through the years. Perhaps they don't have physical descendants to carry themselves on in time, but somehow their aura never quite allows them to disappear.

Sometimes you fear that unless you keep their essence alive through recounting to others something of who they were, they may just vanish forever. But, even so, they return to you...Perhaps another person may not be open to appreciate your attachment to them, but you know that in little moments they will continue to give meaning to your life.

Some forty years ago I met such a singular person when I was in my twenties. The character I have created represents this person who seemed to have made a lasting splash wherever we went in the eighties.

Sometimes her celebrity could even be controversial, but always illuminating in its assumptions and irony. Through the years I have been reminded of this life and couldn't help sharing stories of her to family and friends. Now nearing seventy, I figured I finally had the time to set down some of those stories (which will probably be welcomed by my acquaintances since I have probably become repetitive and they are hoping I will finally get this "out of my system").

Introduction to our character would probably best be seen through the lens of a candle-illuminated glass of wine (or a Manhattan as our character would have enjoyed). Or if you are so inclined, through the essence of "A Winter's Tale" by Brad Jacobsen. Please enjoy chapter ten (perhaps enhanced by the songs mentioned therein as you are invited to observe the "goings on" in that event). The final chapter may be best served by "The Gray Woods" by Brad Jacobsen or "When We Met" by Ryan Stewart. Please enjoy opening the door to your imaginings and invite Tekla in. I know she would love to meet you!

CONTENTS

CHAPTER 1

The Introduction

She sat at a small table surrounded by a couple of wooden captain's chairs. Framing her was a cherrywood arch entry to a great room with a built-in buffet also in cherrywood. A stained-glass piano window brought in filtered sunlight above the buffet, which cast a filtered golden spotlight on Tekla. Her initial aura seemed to cast a rather regal impression, which made her appear as though she was ready to hold court.

Her surroundings denoted ghosts of the old mansion she now inhabited. A mansion once graced by a well-heeled local family living an extravagant lifestyle no doubt enhanced by this once mill-town turned midwestern city. However, it appeared, the collateral damage of local capitalism had probably transformed this residence to the mildly profitable family-run boarding home I now saw. While the bones of class remained, the structure was quite spare in furnishing. Besides Tekla there were twenty-two other residents. I gathered most were here due to chronic mental illness. I found the whole milieu fascinating and ironic. However, I was not comprehending the tragic effects on these inhabitants of being put on a shelf out of site. This was perhaps due to my young perceptions at the time. A little too inquisitive, I began to review a few charts. I found myself fascinated by reviewing the history of one particular individual who had been subjected to a series of hospitals and group settings when family could not tolerate her lifestyle and wished to correct her indiscretion, or at least remove her from public scrutiny.

Interrupting my research, I saw Tekla glance up to size up the latest staff person who now tarried in her court. She appeared just over five feet. The thick lenses framing her visage were oblong and seemed to add a touch of old money to her decidedly ethnic features. She subjected me to a quick study, then snuffed out a lipstick-stained cigarette.

"Darling, how may I address you?" she ventured.

"Jack," I said.

"Excuse I…But I must also know your surname, if you please."

I provided said information.

"You appear quite diplomatic and fetching in your manner. How did you come to dazzle us with that graceful bearing in your step and those large limbs of yours. Please, come sit here, you must have a rest before you expend all your energy; I feel drained just watching you. Let's chat a bit while you revive."

Taken off guard by this, but fascinated by her candor and lack of pretense, I begged off for a short while as I catered to other residents and checked in with the previous shift manager. I couldn't help but inquire about why this lady landed in this setting, but got little response.

When I returned to Tekla she interrogated me a little more. I gleaned that she was here between "more suitable permanent locations." I felt there must be much more to Tekla's story, but I would save that for further exploration.

Then she announced, "Of course all these poor souls have lost their zest for life." I tried not to validate this thought, but I sensed no one else heard, or was interested in the statement anyway. "Of course, none of them probably had the benefit of good 'Nordeast' Polish upbringing like I had. After all, wasn't I the little girl they asked to greet the great Stobachevsky with a sheaf of calla lilies when he appeared in concert here? I mean I made something of myself! Why else had a talent scout from Hollywood singled me out and prevailed upon my dear mother to discuss my future? Poor fellow didn't stand a chance when rebuffed in broken English by my proud mother. I requested the reason why, but she only said I was 'too small.' When I queried why I was 'so small,' she said in Polish 'that was all that was left over.'"

I mustered a chuckle.

Tekla then told me she had been executive secretary to Leif Nielson, a local business mogul, and that she had even ordered flowers for his "Monday and Friday girls." She reveled in the knowledge that she was still invited to related parties and that I might be able "to rub elbows" with said dignitaries if I accompanied her. I asserted that would be quite the occasion, though I doubted this grand privilege would ever materialize.

As time went on I realized that Tekla was not just the classy old bespectacled visage I thought she was. On one occasion I was surprised to encounter quite a different side. As I entered the great room, I witnessed a rather disheveled Tekla who seemed to have a painful-looking bruise on her cheekbone. Staff noted a disappearance last weekend, and a drinking binge was suspected. Furthermore, if too many such episodes occurred, she might be asked to leave.

Luckily however, the following shift I was delighted to see her in her usual state of grooming and stylish garb. In fact, she revealed she had stopped at a another nearby old, converted mansion. Having seen it myself I could attest to its grandeur and charm. It had gone commercial as well and was now the home of the Hoffman Salon. This was a rather snooty establishment where pageboy adorned talent sought to capitalize on the owner's brand of style. I was surprised to discover that Hoffman himself had insisted that Tekla be a drop-in model for his students. In fact, he frequently styled her hair himself. Apparently, I was not the only victim of Tekla's charm and presence. She beckoned me to join her that day and fed me small wrapped chocolate mint squares she obtained from the crystal bowl at Hoffman's. "Darling, I've just received an invite for two to Leif's holiday party by post and I'm counting on you to accompany me there," she bursted.

"Oh well, I couldn't—"

"Nonsense, you'll fit right in, and what's more, you may just be noticed by some very important people! Now you just wear that white shirt and that fetching vest. Come, dear, we'll have such fun!"

"Well…I'll see," I placated.

"Of course, I will need my cane and a buggy"—a wheelchair—"I shall wear that tasteful gown and heels I acquired in Chicago. I know you'll be as proud to be seen on my arm as I am to be seen on yours."

So, as time went on I became rather enamored of my new discovery. However, before long I realized she was quite complex and flawed like the rest of us. She was asked to leave the board and care after a few more drinking episodes. She moved in up the street to a quaint furnished hotel. Her new well-established abode was eccentric and rather over-the-top. It was evocative of a previously ritzy era in which I could easily imagine this character moving comfortably. I entered the hotel, stepping on the lush overstuffed red velvet carpeting. I inquired about her room number and made my way there. Coiffed in a rather disheveled hairstyle once done by Hoffman's own hands and dressed in an open robe, her apartment door agape, I discovered my subject in an inebriated state by a case of liquor. I expressed great concern about her state and drawn appearance. I checked the refrigerator only to discover a few half-eaten doggie bags from nearby restaurants. Panicked and feeling like I may have signed up for more geriatric trouble than I could handle, I pulled her robe together and left, closing the door. Outside I encountered a concerned building manager who asked if I was aware how much alcohol was being delivered to Tekla's apartment. I tried to assure him that I would do all I could to help, but I wasn't sure I had the fortitude.

The next day, with fresh perspective and resolve, I called the local liquor store in hope of finding a little humanitarian empathy for Tekla's plight. I was assured that deliveries would cease. I would now retreat as gracefully as possible from all this drama. But just as I was prepared to abandon ship, Tekla phoned. While not mentioning her recent binge, she was "touched" by my misplaced concern. We "must go to dinner" and discuss the upcoming Leif affair. Ultimately, I succumbed to the moment. I motored us to her suggested venue, the twelfth floor of a well-known downtown department store. We entered the circular ramp to park.

She pointed out the beautiful, if somewhat faded, floral dress she had obtained from some "madame's house of fashion." *As* we disembarked, she announced she must "micturate." I was at a loss for the nearest bathroom, but she merely squatted purposefully between the cars in the ramp as if all fashionable ladies prescribed to this habit. *As* we strolled to the elevator, she cautioned me that I must always walk to her left so I "wasn't auctioning her off to the nearest bidder." Exiting the express elevator, I entered the restaurant with my cane-driven queen of etiquette. After being seated by the hostess who called Tekla by name, we awaited a menu. Before I could get more than a greeting to the waitress, however, our itinerary was plotted by my partner.

"I should like a Manhattan before we survey the menu," she asserted. I resigned myself to a range of possible outcomes as I ordered a rum and Coke for myself.

After Tekla leisurely downed the Manhattan, she "must, of course, have one more." I requested an ice water, which arrived with an elaborately twisted lemon rind. As I admired it, I wondered what kind of compensation I might receive if I was the lemon rind designer here. When dinner was over (or so I thought), Tekla requested a Stinger for her palate. But that wasn't all. "Now we'll have our coffee," she interjected. "And get the young man whatever dessert he craves. I shall have a Haagen-Dazs with Grand Marnier sauce." Spellbound by how much alcohol Tekla could fit in her five-foot frame, I wondered how sporting we would look as we made our exit. As we left, she exhibited her clout with the hostess. "Thanks, Becky, it was truly memorable, and tell the kitchen I appreciate their serving only Haagen-Dazs as I suggested."

We returned to Tekla's apartment as I checked my watch and calculated that my dinner with Tekla averaged two and a half hours.

A Friend and I

Private Mansion now. Was the board and care.

Van Dussen Mansion Home of the Horst Salon

Oak Grove Hotel

CHAPTER 2

The Leif Affair

On the night of the Leif Holiday Party, I was more than a little anxious. I picked up my charge at seven and managed to squeeze the wheelchair into the hatch of the car. Tekla presented with a dark blue dress with a frilly white collar, sporting her best cane. Barely able to manage her heels, I suggested other footwear, but she insisted these shoes had taken her to Chicago and New York and had always worn beautifully. (Thank goodness for wheelchairs or we would never get seated in time).

However, we did manage fairly good time; we located the approximate vicinity of the soiree in the complex. The hotel was quite beautiful, and more than one regally dressed invitee recognized our Secretary Extraordinaire. This list included Leif's wife. Tekla reached back from the hand rest of her buggy to observe, "I guess Monday and Friday won't be present, always was a headache for me to arrange plane tickets for 'never the twain must meet'!" We were ushered into a huge banquet hall with crystal chandeliers and a couple hundred beautifully adorned round tables. I was relieved when we were escorted to a table not too conspicuously near the front. However, perhaps I had underestimated Tekla's star power. The vice president's table spotted her as she was wheeled in on her throne, and "of course" she must be seated nearer to Leif. We joined the VP guests one table away from Leif, and the private accolades ensued over Tekla.

Each table was graced with take-home specially engraved ornament favors with the letters "LN" for each guest. Each table had its own unique floral arrangement. "The help" kept us in wine and breadsticks as speaker after speaker praised the guest of honor. The crowd reveled in the history of his rise from humble street seller to marketing genius. As time evolved, I couldn't help but notice subtle changes in the volume of Tekla's voice as she downed each goblet of courage. As we got closer to the speech we had all assembled for, I noticed the VP excusing himself from our table to speak at the podium. Tekla squeezed my hand as if to focus me more intently. The room quieted; our speaker began to introduce the guest of honor. Forgetting the volume of her voice, Tekla began to weigh in at our table during a quiet moment.

"Well, of course he knew how to make his fortune, he married it," she observed.

Unfortunately, the very bride and Leif's daughter was in earshot. There was a pause at our table, and then few uncomfortable chuckles erupted. I took wing quickly with Tekla's wheelchair as she reached for Leif's engraved ornament.

"Darling, have we been excused?" she queried.

"Just thought you might want a cigarette," I whispered in her good ear. Then I navigated our ship to the nearest doorway, and we entered. The kitchen staff seemed alarmed, but we zoomed through.

"Darling, did we miss our exit?" she remonstrated.

"Well, this is the quickest way to the smoking area," I improvised.

In record time we opened another door, which led to a loading dock. She noted with one arthritic digit raised that the smoking area really could use "a little more ambience." Having little time to be proud of myself for saving the day, Tekla expressed the need to "micturate" again. Not wishing another parking ramp exhibition, I ushered her down a little incline. We followed the perimeter a short distance when we encountered an entrance. We entered and returned to a hall area within ear shot of Leif's speech. Aha, the sign to "Ladies Powder Room" loomed large above me. What luck! However, there was not enough time to retrieve her cane from the car and she insisted, of course, she must walk in under her own volition. The "Ladies Powder Room" really was indeed a "Powder Room." The "micturation process" actually occurred in an adjoining area. I advised Tekla to follow the handrail on the inner wall on the left "sans" mirrored vanities. She could then enter the appropriate chamber for the deed to be accomplished. I brought her buggy as close as possible to the first room. She chuckled a little, grabbed the handrail, and soldiered on with a purposeful wisp of her free hand. Feeling again like I triumphed over the moment, I waited for what seemed to be an eternity.

As I waited, a genteel-looking lady in a shimmering green sequin gown happened upon me.

"Do you belong to that…woman in the powder room?" She brushed off a dust ball from the sequins of her lower dress. "I had to crawl under the cubicle door and unlock it for her." She shot me a reprimanding glance, shifted her gown, and sashayed on.

Waiting for Tekla's take on the adventure as she exited, I was left bereft of an answer. However, we returned to the dining hall, which seemed to have forgotten any indiscretions we may have committed previously. In fact, we seemed to have few groupies now that had taken notice of our misplaced candor. Dinner proceeded as I silently wished that any excess alcohol might be absorbed by solid food and coffee. The mass-produced entrees of fish or chicken arrived as pre-ordered. The meal ended with a parade of servers with extended arms held high with trays of faux Baked Alaska.

After dessert and coffee, Tekla and I exited before the closing speech (probably to mixed revues). I gratefully beckoned her to our final exit. We returned to the relative safety of her abode, and she fell asleep in the middle of a sentence, surrounded by her extravagant couch.

Grateful was I to close the chapter on this mission. Homeward bound!

Fast escape through the kitchen

CHAPTER 3

Time For Tea

I was buoyed by Tekla's indomitable recovery skills when next I saw her. The previous social engagement had not embarrassed her; in fact, it seemed to have validated her own self-worth.

She proudly proclaimed, "Darling, I should like to go to Young's fine department store. Now, I may have not revealed anything to you about the proprietors, but I knew you would be rapt with curiosity. Truth is that they were lovebirds without benefit of marriage; everyone knew, of course. Think of it. Needless to say, they were terribly successful. They created a store that is superlative in every way. I mean it's really a class act! You simply must see it if you hadn't the foresight to see it already."

"Guilty," I pleaded.

So, hoping to avoid any parking ramp episodes or bathroom rescues, I submitted that we would use her buggy, but also bring into the store her cane le jour.

Before we drove downtown, I had charted the course, locating parking nearby, and surveyed the landscape. I was amazed by the exterior gargoyles and appliques on the face of the department store.

Now as we entered the store, I was further amazed by the sales personnel, with their white cotton gloves behind aromatic counters of perfume and makeup. Then the Estee Lauder girl nabbed Tekla and asked to "freshen her face." Tekla hiked herself up on an elevated stool with a little boost from me. Looking a little precarious, but regal, the renovation progressed successfully. Tekla's plumage puffed up and beautiful, we made our way toward the elevator with a flashing neon sign saying, "this car up." Prior to this excursion I hadn't realized there were any elevators that were still commandeered by attendants. Our operator with supple black leather gloves urged us forward. The brass latticework door opened, then closed with us safely inside. A nasal voice signaled "full car," then with a rapid swing of a lever we vaulted rather suddenly toward the heavens. I felt a little queasy from the speed of elevation (and the quick stops to announce each floor and description of its priceless marvels).

Finally, the door opened to "The Fountain Room." Everything was decorated of ivory and pastel green. A rather small, active water fountain with a cupid apparently gave the room credibility. Rows of white tastefully adorned tables adorned with silverware and ashtrays with the fountain logo awaited us. Women of some apparent measure were scattered about.

Most holding burning cigarettes in the required forearm up and slightly tipped back position.

After ingesting little tasteless finger sandwiches and listening to patrons proclaim they simply "couldn't eat another bite," Tekla had the wanderlust again. We must go to "the hab" for drinks. It was a short jaunt and I had never been there. Surprisingly, Tekla thought the place "just peachy" even though the floors were famously covered from empty peanut shells.

Margaritas and endless bowls of legumes were lavished upon the guests. Apparently, Tekla's reputation and tipping prowess had preceded her for the servers flocked to their notorious guest. The servers were extremely attractive, and I found my eye wandering. She simply could not fathom that any of these creatures "could possibly" be gay when suggested. Surprisingly, Tekla imbibed rather conservatively, which was welcomed by her new self-appointed companion. We returned to her chambers as we reviewed our little world with memories a little accentuated by the life (and spirits) we had just ingested.

CHAPTER 4

Salon au Claire de Lune

In a week I returned to Tekla's apartment per her request for a little to-do list she had devised. She motioned me in as she spoke in an interesting dialect to someone on the phone. Seemed to be a little French with some American slang thrown in. "Salon au Claire de Lune," she noted in French. Then, she made excuses to exit the interaction.

"Darling," she said, "I was speaking to Mirlande, an acquaintance. We met in transit one day and hit it off immediately. She seems to be a dear soul and we said we should rendezvous sometime. Well, she gave me an invite to meet up for a little afternoon libation. Isn't that grand? Think of it. I told her we'll—"

"We'll? I'm not sure—"

"Nonsense! It'll be worth your while, unless you already have an engagement," she tested. "And after all, I have exposed you to people who've really arrived, haven't I?"

"All right, let me know the time and directions," I supplicated.

"Natch. I wouldn't steer you wrong." She chuckled.

So, on a weekday before noon we absconded on our pre-determined rendezvous. Passing through downtown from Tekla's apartment, Tekla pointed to a local gay bar.

"That was the Tourist Motel. There was no need to bring luggage to spend the night, quite the destination!" She scowled.

My passenger sent us further down Hennepin, followed by a right on Washington. On to University toward St. Paul, remembering when the old Foshay Tower was the highest vantage point. Onward to 7th Street.

"I really don't know of any French clubs around here," I submitted.

"Turn here."

"Tekla, this is a one-way, and we'd be going the wrong direction."

"Nonsense, if anyone stops us just tell them we're with Leif Nielson." I followed my guide, and finally we came to an unlikely haunt with a weather-beaten sign proclaiming "Moonshine Saloon."

"Are you sure this is it?" I said to my visually impaired guide.

She affirmed, so we parked. She brandished her cane, and we "must tell management they need light to make this place more inviting," she observed.

I led the way as Tekla groped at my arm until her night vision began to improve a little.

"Annie," a voice called out. We finally divined the exact source of our speaker. "Hope you all don't mind me calling you Annie. I never did know Polish, just French and 'merican."

Je suis charme," Tekla fawned (charmingly).

"*Ce n'est rien,*" followed, with a little sucking sound and a spit of snus in a little copper spittoon.

"Disgusting!" Tekla protested. "Someone bring the lady a bottle of water with a twist, not runoff from some lime-ridden tap. Really, I'd do the same thing, poor Mirlande."

Mirlande said something rather inaudible in a slangish French which didn't seem to be table worthy.

"So, Mirlande," I segued, "what part or France do you hail from?"

"T'ain't no France." Then she intimated what sounded like "Port-au-Prince." Tekla seemed left wanting for clarification, but moved on after a server brought a Perrier and a huge bowl of something that smelled wonderful.

Tekla said, "Mirlande, do tell, is that seafood you're having? Oh, I must have a taste!" Mirlande shoved the bowl toward Tekla and me.

"Simply scrum!" Tekla declared. "Jack, it's okay, family style. Just dig in, dear."

"I do love me some chicken feet!" reminisced Mirlande. This missed Tekla's good ear and she asked for clarification of what this delectable morsel was she now masticated.

Mirlande brushed a little grease from her lip and divulged, *"Pattes de Poulet."*

"Oh 'M,' when will you French ever stop coming up with more new words and dishes for we Americans to fathom?"

Mirlande looked puzzled.

So the visit progressed, and Mirlande relayed a little history of the place complete with ghosts and beer glasses sliding down the bar counter. Tekla was transfixed. Tekla declared that we would all meet again.

We returned to Tekla's hotel as she marveled about her acquaintance. "I mean it's a pleasure to meet real people in this world." She squeezed my hand to emphasize her point. "Real people like you!"

Moonshine Saloon now closed. History of ghost sightings.
Still there and even more spooky now.

CHAPTER 5

A Detour

Striding up the walk to Tekla's hotel, I wondered what was in store for us today. Arriving at her apartment I noticed she wore more casual attire than usual.

"Does this scarf lend itself to a little tour in your automobile?" she probed. "I so hoped you could see our dream home."

I affirmed her intentions, and we embarked on our journey. We drove past a few landmarks and discovered a few things that had changed since she dallied there before. She insisted we drive up and down Newton Avenue, where she fully expected we would find Lincoln Del and experience "the best matzo ball soup anywhere," Trying to assure her I had never seen a Lincoln Del in this location, we finally decided it had disappeared from the area when Homewood residents flocked to St. Louis Park. Moving on, down Theodore Wirth Drive, then left a few miles, we were in sight of Cedar Lake. Slight right to the Lake Forest Edition, taking in beautiful winding roads past well-to-do homes in Linden Hills. Right turn at the sign to a short dead-end road.

"There it is, think of it!" she said, fully expecting I would be immediately enthralled. I took in a rather modest but architecturally beautiful rambler with manicured appearance. Not as large as many of the other homes in the area, but quite commanding in its own simplicity. A slanting roof seemed to focus attention to a stone fireplace in front, just off center.

"Ron had Lannon stone brought in from Wisconsin. We designed the floorplan ourselves!" She then walked me through a virtual tour of their dream cottage. "We had a charming housekeeper. Her husband had been a saxophonist for his band; we always remembered him at the holidays. Luella would graciously wear a service uniform on request to the delight of our special guests."

Tekla seemed to drift for a moment, then relayed, "Of course, Ron was my second husband. I met him in later years. Don was my first. He was a football player. They used to call him 'Two Beer Fournier.' I can still see him, with that hat always a little askew. Even his athletic strength couldn't prevent the damage that a steering wheel did to his chest. After the automobile accident, I was with him in the hospital. His heart couldn't hold anymore, and when it collapsed, it was like the report of a gun. Can you imagine?" I tried to, and made my apologies for her terrible loss.

"Of course, I met Ron after his divorce and my loss. He had been a navy man. We often quipped that our election votes were futile since they canceled each other out. He was a dyed-in-the-wool Republican and I was a staunch Democrat. Think of it, I donated his ditty box to the 'Hysterical Society.'" She always called it that. "When I inquired about where it would be displayed, they told me it was safely stored who knows where until it could be honored "appropriately."

"Yes, he was another handsome—and proud—man. So proud he destroyed all pictures of my first husband. So proud he could never tell me he was unable to have children. His sister broke the news to me. I never mentioned it to him all those years later, as he lay dying from cancer. He smoked all the way to the end, but I still miss him."

I looked for a way to comfort or distract her at this moment, but finally Tekla took charge. "Enough of all this gloom!" She raised a Kleenex to her nose as if I wouldn't notice the real reason for its use. "How about a-drive around the lakes?"

"Absotively, posolutely, as the lady would desire!" I tried to hide my own feelings with humor. She chuckled thoughtfully.

"Sometimes I just wish you could meet someone from my family, such a curse to be the little *'dziecko'* of the family. My dear brother Tom kept his suspender pants on the bedpost. He would always say, 'Help yourself to a nickel, my little Kocham.'"

After a tour around the lakes, I returned her to her solitude. She insisted I reach in her purse and help myself to some chocolate mint squares she had obtained from her last Hoffman Salon makeover. I thanked her and left.

CHAPTER 6

In Search of Cocktails

On a Sunday I was off from work, Tekla had the wanderlust. "Darling, I should like to take refreshments," she proposed. Feeling more comfortable with Tekla's recent alcoholic self-discipline, I drove to her first suggestion, not open....I suggested another, but it didn't serve alcohol. As we continued on, we spotted a bar with a large football above the door. I felt this place was way too conspicuous for us and didn't wish to darken its door.

"This will be fine, even if it is a little casual," she insisted. "You really must be more at ease. Your big shoulders can handle it."

I prepared myself, and presented my fetching Hoffman model to those inside as we entered under the football-adorned entrance. She commented again about poorly lit establishments, but I found refuge in that anonymity. Past the bar area with regulars watching a game. On to cushy booths in earshot of other patrons, I seated Tekla.

Waiting a bit, then our server provided us with drinks. The afternoon went fairly well until I noticed Tekla's voice began to increase in volume again.

"Darling, now that I understand you are only 'half-a-loaf,' I must inquire as to what two men do for diversion." I realized Tekla wanted the intimate scoop on my physical encounters. Panicking, I reached over the table to whisper in her good ear that while I would like to enlighten her, a sports bar might not be the best place.

"After all," I whispered, "I wouldn't ask what you and Don did together."

"So you are inquiring what we did in the throes of passion?…Well, at first there was generally foreplay, which usually included—"

"Tekla, I really didn't want to—"

However, she continued to outline a litany of steps which led to the ultimate fruition of her happy place.

I tried to check peripherally to see how our nearby sports patrons were receiving our true confessions at first, then I laser focused on a logical time table for our socially acceptable escape. Pay the bill, avoid any questions about who would win the game in case anyone asked since I didn't know who was playing, enter the end zone as nonchalantly as possible, and don't look back after exiting under the football.

After a quiet ride back to Tekla's, we slithered into the hotel, past Tiffany lamps on the overstuffed carpet to madame's chambers. I helped batten down the hatches, and took my 'half-a-loaf' elsewhere.

Enough Said

CHAPTER 7

Where to for Luncheon

One day around noon while we were returning from a doctor's appointment, Tekla announced a "most gnawing hunger." Not far from the Gay Ninety's on Hennepin, I decided we would try "luncheon" there, since I knew drinks would be required. I thought she might be just campy enough to fit in. So, my bouffant-crowned companion and I entered this wonderland of hanging buggies with mannequins dressed in nineteenth-century garb.

Taking it all in through her thick spectacles, Tekla proclaimed, "What whimsical fun, darling! Kind of like a carnival, isn't it?"

"Yes, I suppose it might qualify," I conjectured. As with other such establishments, the server fawned over my charge. As a quiet aside he asked me at one point if she was a celebrity. I assured him she was no less the executive secretary of "a business genius."

"I have to know who does her hair; I want the same do for our Gala Ball," he pleaded. I told him she had an exclusive designer who was not accepting new clients. "A shame!" he demurred.

We embarked on Tekla's usual routine. First and second Manhattan, leisurely meal with minutia about family members, history of Tekla's exploits, including mention of her invitation for wine at the rectory with priests from her mother's dear church northeast. It was great fun until they would venture into her solemn assertion that there "really was no hereafter" and she fully intended to sleep quietly in the earth someday. Tekla noted she was always welcomed back, however.

Main course, commenting on my eating too fast and the need to enjoy the whole masticating thing. Food was "scrum," Stinger for the palate, coffee and ice cream, but no Haagen-Dazs available with her Grand Marnier. Sit through her summoning the head cook to discuss the benefits of serving said ice-cream.

"I can't remember a more surprising luncheon," Tekla declared. "And I thought I knew all the best destinations. Darling, you've been holding out on me! You really use your head for more than finishing off your neck! What a scamp!"

"I've been known to scare up a little attention when I'm with a proper guest. Thanks for noticing," I interjected. "Shall we exit before we create too big a stir?"

"Yes, darling, before they show us the door," she quipped.

CHAPTER 8

French Onion Soup Anyone?

When next I saw Tekla, she suggested luncheon at Rudolph's. She proclaimed she knew the owner. "Darling, he's a charming Greek. I think it would be good for your social resume, don't you…Well, of course it would."

So we braved the winter elements and proceeded down Franklin Avenue in Uptown to the home of unrivaled barbecue and celluloid ghosts from the talkie period. Walls of Hollywood demigods surrounded us as we entered, including Rudolph Valentino, of course. Room by room led to more current legends as well. Tekla paused at glammed-up androgenous prints of David Bowie and Mick Jagger. "I do so love clowns, don't you? At our dream home I collected ceramic clowns for our mantle. I should like a print of that one with the red grease paint on the mouth and the colorful neck scarf."

Sitting in a booth, we embarked on an episode from the life and times of Tekla. A newly seated pair of young women sat opposite our booth wearing tattoos and safety pin earrings with spiked hair.

Tekla commented, "It appears her hairdresser uses an eggbeater to fashion that style. I surely hope he didn't set her back too much."

I whispered close to her good ear that she needed to be a little more quiet.

Our French onion soup came in little four-footed pots. Cheese dripping over the rim. As we talked, a string of cheese became connected like an umbilical cord from the bowl to her mouth. I wished I had a small scissor, but settled for a butter knife and fork as I nondescriptly severed the cord. Tekla never missed a beat with her monologue.

The restaurant owner happened by, but didn't escape Tekla's arthritic talons. He didn't seem to recognize our cause c'ele'bre immediately but managed a "so-o good to see you again." (I wanted to tip him.)

Our outing continued as we adhered religiously to Tekla's dining routines and carried on with our usual table talk. At one point Tekla seemed on a mission about a theater outing she took in recently.

"Darling, I took a cab to see that movie. The one that won the academy award, that *Deer Hunter* I believe it was. Couldn't finish it. I mean it was disgusting! I had to ask the concession girl if management should continue airing it. What has happened to motion pictures? Gloria Swanson would be aghast!"

(I thought we might ask her in person since her visage peered down at us from her perch on the wall).

Returning to Tekla's confines, we secured her for the night.

She was still processing how the world was becoming a different place around her, but her immediate world was comforting and warm as the snow fell quietly outside her window between the well-appointed curtains.

Rudolph's now defaced with graffiti

*Building mostly empty but mirrored
image I obtained with flashlight*

CHAPTER 9

Spring Thaw

Tekla and I continued to belong to our own "mutual admiration society" as we wondered through many adventures, though to others we may have seemed a little petty around the edges. But, I began to be pulled in other directions due to romances and other responsibilities. Now trained as a nurse, I realized I was drawn to other interesting personas (such as Tekla became in my life). I seemed particularly drawn to those who perhaps no longer had much family. Beings like myself and Tekla who never wanted (or had) children to carry themselves on.

Tekla had sometimes annoyed me because of her single mindedness and focus on Tekla's history. As we discussed all things Tekla, one day I mentioned my recent connection to an elderly acquaintance I helped to rescue from her own apartment when it became apparent that some form of dementia was taking over her life. I relayed how Penny seemed to have been interrupted by mild agitation at first, then hoarding ensued.

Stopping by a rack of apartment guides, she would take all of them. Bus schedules also disappeared en masse when she happened by them. She accumulated road atlases from any state she could find. Perhaps all of these things represented her previous more carefree life of travel and adventure. It seemed like now she had only the freedom to look at options and places she could plan or pretend to venture to.

Tekla related, "Darling, you shouldn't trouble yourself with creatures like that. I went to Rochester Mayo when this curse of arthritis started to cramp my style. I spoke with doctors and was told to avoid chocolates and stay away from things and people who upset me. Best advice I ever got."

Remembering my sometimes harrowing experiences with Tekla, I ventured, "Perhaps I never would have known you if I never took a chance. Sometimes I feel that my history and other acquaintances are unimportant to you. I've met Mirlande and former business colleagues of yours, but sometimes I feel like my history gets lost in yours. Don't you think that sometimes I might like to broaden your world a little?"

"Oh darling, I had no clue you had been so deprived…poor dear. I tell you what, let's plan a little social experiment. I'll invite Mirlande and you invite that…Penelope, is it?" she probed.

"How about that marvelous place you took me to with all the buggies hanging from the ceiling?"

"The Gay Nineties? I'm not sure if that—"

"Oh, nonsense, I think it's charming. Puts you in your own turf and I can size up the competition." She chuckled.

"Penny is not the competition!"

"There I am, stepping on your pride again…forgive me?"

"All right…you're pardoned. Guess we've embarked on some unlikely situations before. I'll invite Penny, you phone Mirlande. Do you think she's ready for this?"

"Leave Mirlande to me," she asserted.

Tekla phoned Mirlande and pressed the speaker phone button on her Princess phone.

"Bonjour; cherie."

"Bonjour, mon petite coquin...Just let me get rid o' this cat. Diable, go find that mouse you scared up."

"Aren't you a kidder! I know your housekeeper wouldn't allow such an atrocity. You remember Jack, of course?"

"Oh, that one."

Tekla revealed our plan.

"Huh, I heard o' that place, *'nellie garcons.'*"

"Aren't you precious. I don't have my French dictionary handy, dear." Tekla arranged a time and announced "our car" would arrive for her at nine.

"Honey, no need, I'll bus it. You know people look like me fought to get a seat, and I won't give away all they went through."

"Aren't you a revelation!" Tekla declared. After the *"au reviors,"* Tekla observed, "I think she'll be captivated, don't you?"

"I think she'll definitely be captive at least," I offered.

CHAPTER 10

The Grand Experiment

On the night of our "outing" I exited my newly washed chariot and completed the walk to Tekla's dressed in a pink golf shirt with the alligator logo so popular for the time. Knocking first, then announcing myself, I opened the door to a Tekla never before revealed to me in a daring black suit and white tie.

"What, no dress? Is this a scene from that *Morocco* movie and this must be Marlena Dietrich who stands before me?" I observed.

"Oh, heavens no! She was of the enemy country's extraction!" She scowled.

"How can you say that? She sheltered German and French exiles. She was a real patriot," I reminded.

"I would rather be Kathryn Hepburn if pants must be worn! I met her casually in New England when visiting Ron's people. I knew she wore the pants in that relationship, and I forgive her for breaking up a proper Catholic marriage. I thought her even more beautiful than on the movie screen. No need to disguise those beautiful freckles. Though I would have admonished her about the pants," she admitted.

Then she recounted, "Darling, I mentioned to Hoffman about our plans; he insisted I make a bold statement. You can imagine my surprise when he called in his crew and I was measured, prodded, and surveyed by his henchmen! I was made to return the following day and presented with this 'getup.' He wanted to alter my crown as well, but I stood firm. I knew you would agree."

Although I recognized the irony of her bouffant in contrast to the desired gender statement, I assured her that her tresses were inseparable from her persona. She told Mirlande about her makeover as well and Mirlande was in preparation for the event too.

I had decided to pick up Tekla before Penny that evening to avoid Tekla's fragile ego being slighted. I reminded her of Penny's deficits and expected her to be compassionate. Stopping at the assisted living, I signed out my new friend. Of course, Tekla must be in the front, so I strapped in Penny in the back seat.

"Thank you thank you thank you," she said. I complimented her on her mismatched color scheme and painted nails. Tekla reached over and squeezed my hand, but kept mum. Penelope seemed to marvel about the sights and repeated the words on signs she saw.

Tekla turned toward the back seat and inquired, "Dear, how do you like your residence?"

"Stuffy people, good food. I like your hat!" Tekla hadn't heard this exactly and mentioned her hair was done exclusively at Hoffman's.

"That's nice that's nice," was the response.

Arriving at the Nineties parking lot, I paid Swede (the lot attendant) and grabbed Tekla's cane and buggy. I found that Penny enjoyed pushing the wheelchair, and, with a minimum of direction, we entered the establishment as I opened the door.

A formidable bouncer named Sal scrutinized the latest entrants. Sal, known for removing dancers from the dance floor just because he could, now looked for telltale violations of protocol. Luckily, my flock was not wearing open-toed shoes or other indications that might portend anti-patron intentions. If anything, Tekla's ambivalently contrived uniform/hair caused him to pause momentarily before waving us in to face further (probationary) asylum.

Having arrived just before the onslaught of wall-to-wall gay "boomers" just liberated and turned loose in a candy store to the strains of disco music, we found a nice table close to the dance floor. The dinner menu now closing, drinks were now the only form of nourishment. Breaking with her tradition, Tekla suggested Chablis for our table. I signaled approval to the waiter, but exempted Penny to prevent drug or memory interactions and suggested a Shirley Temple, which she seemed to endorse. After drinks were served and created a little buzz, I enjoyed the dancing golden reflections the candlelit flame imprinted on the glasses and lined profile of Tekla's face.

As we sat at table, a proud visage in a man's black dashiki shirt with the Haitian colors stepped toward us. A partially shaded face peered out at us from under a wide-brimmed straw hat that couldn't disguise the angular face of Mirlande. A slightly unnerved Tekla studied the face and attire through thick lenses, and then relayed, "What a darling Carnivale costume, Mirlande! No doubt someone has been to the French Quarter at Mardi Gras and never told me, you scamp!"

Mirlande glanced at me and shrugged her shoulders as she found her empty chair.

"Well, of course only your lovely complexion could pull off such a radiant splash of color! I have always gravitated to more traditional hues myself," Tekla declared.

Just then Penelope blurted, "Lah-di-dah, lah-di-dah!"

To this Tekla replied, "Have we just sampled a bit of Penelope's wit?

"She's a poet and she don't know it," jibed Penelope in monotone.

"Doesn't know it," corrected Tekla.

"Sorry sorry sorry," offered Penelope.

"My darling girl, let's have a truce, shall we? "Why don't we go to the ladies' room. If you could push my buggy, I'll navigate. We'll let Jack and Mirlande catch up."

"Are you girls really up to it?" I worried.

"I'm sure Penny would love to push me around a bit," she quipped.

As they sailed into the sunset, Mirlande remarked, "One's crazy, I think the other one's fakin'…I still care about that crazy one though. I've known some men back home, and maybe one or two women I'll admit. I want to know that woman. She a little older, but she's got a beautiful soul. And she smart, don't let her fool you!"

Whoa, I thought, *is she really telling me what I think she is telling me?*

Before long, the unlikely adventurers returned to the nest.

Tekla now announced that Penny and she had discovered they had a geographic connection. "Think of it, we both hail from Nordeast!" she boasted. "Small world, small world" echoed Penny.

"Of course, we went to Holy Cross, and my dear friend's family tithed at St. Helwig's, isn't it a providence?"

The night progressed as the club crowded and the steady beat of disco competed with strobe lights to catch us seeing one another in snapshots. Our expressions alternated between delight and sometimes "deer caught in the headlights." The anthem "I Will Survive" caused gasps from the audience as the masses responded to Gloria Gaynor's call. Penny was taken over and reached for my hand as she left her chair. I followed her lead to the stage as we gave in and were like puppets directed by imaginary strings radiating from the ceiling. Then I had to return Penny to home base before she overextended herself.

I realized Tekla was a little miffed when we returned to our perch, but she chuckled tolerantly. As the disc jockey sensed he was losing control of the floor, he announced a ballad he hoped might calm the fever and encourage slow dancers. The strains of "La Vie en Rose" by Grace Jones began as our Mirlande surprised Tekla and held out a hand to her. Tekla giggled with some apprehension, but empowered by the moment and her Chablis, she reluctantly stood up as I tried to intercede subtly to prevent any mishap. While relying on Mirlande's steady arm, she signaled to me she would only venture to the perimeter of the floor with a wisp of her free hand.

Then the already thinned-out dancers on the floor shifted to let the unlikely dance pair be spotlighted as I beckoned, "No dipping, Mirlande!" Mirlande smirked as though she read more into my admonishment than I intended and tipped her head dress in my direction. The two profiles dressed in unplanned color-coordinated gear caused a little stir in the middle of the loud din of the crowd. We overheard someone remark "Aren't they cute!" Then questioning what gender they were before returning to the horseshoe bar.

As the music began to quell, the DJ taunted the less faint of heart again and continued with the jungle beat of Grace Jones with "Slave to the Rhythm." Seeing our table starting to fade a little, I proposed closing out the night before last call for alcohol and the lights turned up to expose the reality of our well-aged countenances. As I tried and failed to dissuade Mirlande from boarding the last #12 to St. Paul and riding with us instead, Tekla, Penny, and I dredged up enough energy to return to our carriage before it changed back into a pumpkin, or someone lost a glass geriatric slipper.

CHAPTER II

Debriefing at Murray's

Having not heard from Tekla since our last adventure, on a sunny spring morning I called her for an update. She would fill me in at luncheon. She suggested Murray's (Home of the "Silver Butter Knife Steak") downtown. She informed me that it was a common watering hole when she worked at Faegre Benson as a clerical secretary. The building face advertised its famous specialty motto, just under the commanding lights of the Murray's sign. Tekla and I entered the beautifully lit restaurant, which appeared much larger inside due to a wall of mirrored tiles to the right. Reflections of candle-lit tables illuminated the modest crowd inside as I noted the mirrored spectacle of the two of us singularly mismatched in height and era as we strutted in.

We were seated at a table by the host as I surveyed interesting little contraptions at each table, apparently battery driven and plastic with arched handles. A button in the center of the base caused the arch to light up in green with the word "Service" when pressed. I noticed an array of uniformed staff waiting on tables and busing dishes around us.

Behind Tekla I observed an older woman with an unpretentious dress. She was un-uniformed in contrast to other staff. She wore glasses and a pragmatic hairstyle of silver/gray. As I talked with Tekla, I occasionally glanced over Tekla's shoulder as the woman cleaned the glass which covered the white tablecloth of each vacated table. She had obviously worked during her life, as her slightly bent posture showed the gracious loyalty of her labors. Tekla noticed my distraction at one point and inquired about my lack of attention. Just then, the woman came round Tekla's chair to greet Tekla.

"Mrs. Murray, how good to see you again," Tekla responded.

"And I hope this day finds you in good health, my dear," Mrs. Murray countered. She paused a little to show respect to her loyal customer, then excused herself and entered the kitchen area at her usual rapid clip.

"What a dear soul, think of it. Carrying on after her life's partner gave his all to this wonderful restaurant. When I look at her, I see my own dear mother, humble and unassuming in her job on this earth," she observed.

She then tried to reconcile how fate had chosen to spare her "childbearing hips" from their motherly function. I assured her that her life had a rich history, caring for two husbands, demonstrating how a woman of the world dared to make her own way in business and lifestyle.

Unmoved by my words, she continued, "Well, let me catch you up. So I returned my wardrobe to Hoffman's the other day. They were terribly interested in our 'goings on' the other night when I filled them in on the gory details. I drew a little crowd of his cronies. Do you know that they were most interested in Mirlande's attentions toward me? They asked if I was 'flattered' by her behavior! I assured them I grew up in a Polish home where girls prepped together before dances so that men could have a proper dance partner. I let them know that I was 'not of that ilk'!

"So naturally I felt it important to discuss appearances with Mirlande, just in case she was getting the wrong idea about our friendship. I told her after all the name Tekla means 'God's glory' in Polish. She relayed to me that her name had island origins and meant 'black bird.' She imagined that if I went to God's glory, she would be the little bird flying up to greet me! I assured her she would find me at St. Mary's Cemetery if she chose to see me in repose. Can you imagine!"

"How sweet!" I retorted. I tried to smooth Tekla's ruffled feathers and assured her that Mirlande meant no harm and would always respect her intentions anyway. She seemed placated for the moment. I told her I regretted that she felt that way about people of that "ilk" and that it seemed personal to me. Then I asked Tekla if she ever felt any regrets herself.

Thinking for a moment, she interjected, "Well, I guess I regret I may have caused you to think I really didn't know that 'Dame Edna' character on TV was really a man in a dress." Knowing I wasn't satisfied with her response, she tried again. "I regret not gaining a college degree." Then she realized I sought more from her. She began to tear up behind those magnified lenses. She began to tell me about a childhood regret.

"When I was a child, my dear mother requested my brother Tom and I dispose of a feral litter of kittens. I so trusted my family that I never thought better of it. I was told that it would be necessary for us to tie them in a flour sack and drop them off the bridge into the river. At the time, I did so, thinking it was 'a lark.' Can you imagine? To this day I am angry at my dear mother. I now wish I could collect those kittens and let them know I never meant to hurt them." She looked to me for solace, though my face registered shock at first. Now I regretted my probing. I let her know that as children, we must rely upon adults to guide us through and she was never at fault. However, it was good to see that this proud woman could emote her feelings and release her inner child.

Before leaving Murray's, we were able to laugh again about some of our exploits. I felt an honest connection I hadn't felt before to this little survivor of life, and admiration for her indomitable nature.

CHAPTER 12

Final Portal

Tekla would ultimately have to resign herself to life in a care center as her dependencies would dictate. Mirlande had gone before, which seemed to affect Tekla more than I had imagined. Penny continued to live for a long time. Perhaps her only means of travel had been the reason.

She marched incessantly and seemed interested even in the sun, of which she was heard to remark "what a beautiful light." Tekla lived in more than one facility, due to her insistence on keeping her freedom to smoke cigarettes, sleep in the nude as she had always done, and leave by cab whenever she desired a Manhattan. She grieved over losing her mink coat due to "light fingers," which I would have warned her about if I'd known it was in her closet. We still went to some Leif affairs, including a Bob Hope dinner, though she began to feel rather invisible at such events.

She landed at a facility that put her up against a final protagonist: "Miss Oglesby," "the sergeant," a nurse by training who could sniff out a cigarette stash from one hundred yards.

She always suspected Tekla had obtained black market cigarettes from me. If Tekla returned to the home with alcohol her breath, of course she "must be meeting me" somewhere. I was asked to remove all stylish shoes with heels for her safety, which I never did.

My last unannounced visit to the facility found her room empty, with her bed stripped, telling me of her final escape from the confines of her arthritic body. "Miss Oglesby" semi-scolded me for being "reachable" by phone.

I was told which mortuary was called. One of Tekla's favorite dresses was sent along. I knew there weren't any family members to reach (at least according to Tekla). Turned out she really didn't have a plot at St. Mary's with other family members, so she would repose at Fort Snelling Cemetery as the navy widow of her second husband. A mortuary service before burial advertised in both twin city papers brought out some from Leif's company. I was criticized for not recruiting more professionals or friends who knew her. I provided many photos of her pasted to a board at the mortuary.

Because of how this all transpired, it seemed rather an out-of-body experience for me. Perhaps I would grieve later, or maybe not since she seemed to have a long, full, stimulating life to the end.

After the "service" and trip to the cemetery, I returned home. Maybe I was grieving for I just wanted to sleep. Into that welcome ether of comfort between dreaming and the real world, I was a willing traveler. I seemed to drift peacefully off, until I was stirred by a loud voice.

"Darling, have I missed my exit?" A woman of small stature presented from the mist. She carried a Gold Medal flour sack, which seemed to be squirming with movement. Eventually one kitten clawed up to the top of the sack and peered out at me as if she already knew who I was.

"What a lark," I breathed.

TEKLA'S TYPICAL LUNCHEON AT OAKGRILLE ROOM/DAYTON'S 12TH FLOOR (CIRCA 1984)

Manhattan and repeat.

APPETIZER COURSE

Popover served with cup of Cream of Wild Rice soup
(or Seafood Bisque) served in pewter bowl with handle.

MAIN COURSE

Oakgrille Meatloaf with Pine Nuts (Alternate
Choice: Crab Salad with second popover).
Stinger. (and repeat if desired)

DESSERT

Coffee and Haagen-Dazs served
with Gran Marnier sauce

www.ingramcontent.com/pod-product-compliance
Lightning Source LLC
Chambersburg PA
CBHW051554120626
46551CB00013B/1517